GRACE NICHOLS was born in Georgetown, Guyana, where she grew up and worked, among other things, as a reporter and freelance journalist. She came to Britain in 1977 and since then has published a number of children's books which include a collection of her own poems *Come On In To My Tropical Garden* (1988) and a black poetry anthology. Her first book of poems for adults, *i is a long memoried woman*, was winner of the 1983 Commonwealth Poetry Prize. *The Fat Black Woman's Poems* (1984) and her novel *Whole of a Morning Sky* (1986) are published by Virago. Grace Nichols is currently working on a new cycle of poems for which she was awarded an Arts Council bursary. She lives in Sussex with the poet John Agard and her daughter Lesley.

Lazy Thoughts of a Lazy Woman is a sensuous, witty and provocative new collection. Here are poems of laid-back and not-so-laid-back musings, sagas and spells, thoughts on greasy kitchens and patriarchal theology, bikinis and Caribbean migration. But there are moments of poignancy and loss too – as Grace N   ·ky celebration of her ow

D1369130

For my brother, Dennis

Grace Nichols

LAZY
THOUGHTS
OF A LAZY
WOMAN

and other poems

VIRAGO

Published by VIRAGO PRESS Limited 1989
20–23 Mandela Street, Camden Town, London NW1 0HQ

A CIP record for this title is available from the British Library

Typeset by Rowland Phototypesetting Limited,
Bury St Edmunds, Suffolk
Printed in Great Britain by Cox and Wyman Limited, Reading, Berkshire

Contents

one

two

One

Dust

Dust has a right to settle
Milk the right to curdle
Cheese the right to turn green
Scum and fungi are rich words.

Grease

Grease steals in like a lover
over the body of my oven.
Grease kisses the knobs
of my stove.
Grease plays with the small
hands of my spoons.
Grease caresses the skin
of my table-cloth,
Getting into my every crease.
Grease reassures me that life
is naturally sticky.

Grease is obviously having an affair with me.

The Body Reclining

(With a thought for Walt)

I sing the body reclining
I sing the throwing back of self
I sing the cushioned head
The fallen arm
The lolling breast
I sing the body reclining
As an indolent continent

I sing the body reclining
I sing the easy breathing ribs
I sing the horizontal neck
I sing the slow-moving blood
Sluggish as a river
In its lower course

I sing the weighing thighs
The idle toes
The liming* knees
I sing the body reclining
As a wayward tree

I sing the restful nerve

Those who scrub and scrub
incessantly
corrupt the body

Those who dust and dust
incessantly
also corrupt the body

And are caught in the asylum
Of their own making
Therefore I sing the body reclining

*West Indian expression for standing around,
idling away the time.

Who Was It?

Who was it I wonder
introduced the hairless habit?
I have an interest
though I will not shave the armpit

No Gillette
I will not defoliage my forests

Also, let the hairline of the bikini
Be fringed with indecency
Let 'unwanted body hair' straggle free

O Mary Cant
O Estee Laud
O Helena Frankinstein

With Apologies to Hamlet

To pee or not to pee
That is the question

Whether it's sensibler in the mind
To suffer for sake of verse
The discomforting slings
Of a full and pressing bladder
Or to break poetic thought for loo
As a course of matter
And by apee-sing end it.

In Spite of Me

In spite of me
the women in me
slip free
of the charmed circle
of my moulding

Look at Graceful, eh!
long skirts, legs crossed
all smiles
articulating ethnic attentiveness
'Graceful is as graceful is,'
I mock, but Graceful
just goes on being graceful

And Indiscreet
who can stop Indiscreet
from acting indiscreet
wearing her womb on her sleeve
telling the details of her sullied
secrets. Her moves, her searches
her tiresome cosmic wetness.

Obsessional at least
has the good sense
to stay put at home
head tied, cloth soaked in lemon juice,
to keep her thoughts at bay
Obsessional, Obsessional please . . .

Dissatisfied
is really too dissatisfied.
Since she can't change
the course of the rains
or make it possible for people
to feed their children,
she won't do anything. Not even
crawl out of her dressing gown

Focused, dear, dear Focused
is at the typewriter inside –
busy, remote, impatient –
(especially with telephone interruptions)
Focused wants to be left alone
to delve into life
to come up with life
to serve up life
raw, stewed down or evoked

Reassuring, of course,
will do everything
cooking, cleaning,
urging everyone to vitamins
and a balance of meals

Complexity goes off to be
Aaaaaahhh in spite of me
the women in me . . .
                    slip free.

The Decision

In restaurants he fed her
In bed said how he loved her
but she decided to leave him
because he was squeamish

Now she has a new lover
who doesn't feed her
or tell her he loves her
but who buries his face
in plain curiosity of her taste

And tells her how good she is O
And tells her how good she is.

Wherever I Hang

I leave me people, me land, me home
For reasons, I not too sure
I forsake de sun
And de humming-bird splendour
Had big rats in de floorboard
So I pick up me new-world-self
And come, to this place call England
At first I feeling like I in dream –
De misty greyness
I touching de walls to see if they real
They solid to de seam
And de people pouring from de underground system
Like beans
And when I look up to de sky
I see Lord Nelson high – too high to lie

And is so I sending home photos of myself
Among de pigeons and de snow
And is so I warding off de cold
And is so, little by little
I begin to change my calypso ways
Never visiting nobody
Before giving them clear warning
And waiting me turn in queue
Now, after all this time
I get accustom to de English life
But I still miss back-home side
To tell you de truth
I don't know really where I belaang

      Yes, divided to de ocean
      Divided to de bone

Wherever I hang me knickers – that's my home.

Dead Ya Fuh Tan

If me na been come ya
Me na been know
People a dead ya fuh tan

Dem a lie on rock
Dem a lie on sand
People a dead ya fuh tan

Dem a buy sunbed
Dem a buy lotion
People a dead ya fuh tan

Dem a bare dem breast
Dem a bare dem bum
People a dead ya fuh tan

If me na been come ya
Me na been know
People a dead ya fuh tan

Anyway dem can ketch de sun
Anyway dem can ketch a brown
People a dead ya fuh tan.

Wiping the Kalahari

The sun casts the bronze in Benin
in the shrines there are iron-Gods
and iron-things

The amazon woman rides out
she has an armour
where a breast should be

The masai plugs
the blood-hole
of his holy beast

The stone pillars
of Axum, are upheld
A cloud of locusts descends

I'm in the desert
wiping the Kalahari
from my mouth

And all is well with my world of icons.

Because She Has Come

Because she has come
with geometrical designs
upon her breasts

Because she has borne five children
and her belly is criss-crossed
with little tongues of fire

Because she has braided her hair
in the cornrow, twisting it upwards
to show her high inner status

Because she has tucked
a bright wrap
about her Nubian brownness

Because she has stained her toes
with the juice of the henna
to attract any number of arrant males

Because she has the good sense
to wear a scarab
to protect her heart

Because she has a pearl
in the middle
of her lower delta

Give her honour
Give her honour, you fools,
Give her honour.

Eve

Of all the women haunting
the thin pages of the Bible
I would have to give it to Eve.

Virgin Mary got stuck with a permanent halo
and an inconceivable bundle.
Other Mary followed Christ about
too much like a refugee.
Cooking Martha should have tossed the salad
in the direction of the beatific pair.
Veiled Salome danced the head off the baptist
but couldn't have been very bright.
Wily Delilah managed to get herself unwiled.
Reaping Ruth was far too obliging.
Lot's wife . . . what can I say about her?

No, of all the women haunting
the thin pages of the Bible,
it would have to be Eve – ingenuous Eve
who not only came back with the apple
but also with the eel of the first menses.
Newly hatched. Coyly clasped.

Winter-Widow

The winter-widow's at it again.
Screwing her icicle heels
down to the bone.
Tossing back her icy veil,
Planting her burning kisses,
Leaving a rake of frosty finger-blades.

O pity the winter-widow whose autumn-husband
Has died a brown and leafy death.

On Poems and Crotches

(For the poet, ntozake shange)

just tinkin bout/
how hot it isht/
tween yo crotch/
isht enuf/
to make you rush/
to rite a poem/

For poems are born
in the bubbling soul of the crotch.
Poems rise to marry good old Consciousness.
Poems hug Visionary-Third-Eye.
Kiss Intellect.
Before hurrying on down
to burst their way through the crotch.

Women who love their crotches
will rise
higher and higher, past Ravel's Bolero
Will hover on blue mountain peaks
Will drink black coffee
sweetened with magnolia milk

Will create out of the vast silence.

On Stars

Stars are the nipples
of angels
pressed against the face
of heaven.

On Lucy

A bundle of bones
A bundle of premises

The archeologist
Who unearths our first little African Mother
Unearths me, and you too.

Spell Against Too Much
Male White Power

There is too much male white power at loose in the world
There is too much male white power at loose in the world

The smell of Pretoria
The breath of the Pentagon
The eye of the Kremlin

How can I trap it
How can I embalm it
How can I roll it up
like a burial shroud
and put it away
Or at least

How can I persuade it
How can I dissuade it
How can I dissipate it
and spread it thin thin
across my loaf
which of course
would have to be eaten

There is too much male white power at loose in the world
There is too much male white power at loose in the world

How can I cull it
How can I curb it
How can I muzzle the hound
Or at least

How can I bemuse it
How can I confuse it
and like the tower of Babel
bring it all down

O I am a cutter of cataracts
A salter of tongues

There is too much male white power at loose in the world
There is too much male white power at loose in the world

How can I rebound
the missiles and rockets
How can I confound
multinational octopuses
Or at least

How can I remove the 'Big Chiefs'
from the helm
How can I put them to sit on beaches
quiet, sea-gazing, retired old men.

To Which?

To which river
do my veins owe their tributaries

To which ancient earth
do my toes owe their feel

To which forest
does my fanny owe its allegiance

    Songhay Songhay Songhay

Even Tho

Man I love
but won't let you devour

even tho
I'm all watermelon
and starapple and plum
when you touch me

even tho
I'm all seamoss
and jellyfish
and tongue

Come
leh we go to de carnival
You be banana
I be avocado

Come
leh we hug up
and brace-up
and sweet one another up

But then
leh we break free
yes, leh we break free

And keep to de motion
of we own person/ality.

Love

Love is not a grindstone
constantly grinding
wearing down to bone

Love is not an interlocking
deadlock
of inseparable flesh
or a merging of metals
to smooth alloy

Love is a sunshawl
that keeps the beloved warm

Even the undeserving
love floods
risking all.

On Receiving a Jamaican Postcard

Colourful native entertainers
dancing at de edge of de sea
a man-an-woman combination
choreographing
de dream of de tourist industry

de two a dem in smiling conspiracy
to capture dis dream of de tourist industry

an de sea blue
an de sky blue
an de sand gold fuh true

an de sea blue
an de sky blue
an de sand gold fuh true

He staging a dance-prance
head in a red band
beating he waist drum
as if he want to drown she wid sound
an yes, he muscle looking strong

She a vision of frilly red
back-backing to he riddum
exposing she brown leg
arcing like lil mo
she will limbo into de sea

Anything fuh de sake of de tourist industry
Anything fuh de sake of de tourist industry

Ode to My Bleed

Red warm
or livery
Shocking pink
or autumny

I will not part
with my cyclic bleed
my soft seed

Month after month
it tells me who I am
                    reclaiming me
Even as the tides
reclaim the sands

It reminds me of birth
It reminds me of death
It reminds me of the birth in death
                    of seasons
The moon's bright pull
The first primeval fire
lit in the forest temple

Where I watched
O so long ago.

My Black Triangle

My black triangle
sandwiched between the geography of my thighs

is a bermuda
of tiny atoms
forever seizing
and releasing
the world

My black triangle
is so rich
that it flows over
on to the dry crotch
of the world

My black triangle
is black light
sitting on the threshold of the world
overlooking
all my deep probabilities

And though
it spares a thought for history
my black triangle
has spread beyond his story
beyond the dry fears of parch-ri-archy

Spreading and growing
trusting and flowing
my black triangle
carries the seal of approval
of my deepest self.

Two

Abra-Cadabra

My mother had more magic
in her thumb
than the length and breadth
of any magician

Weaving incredible stories
around the dark-green senna brew
just to make us slake
the ritual Sunday purgative

Knowing when to place a cochineal poultice
on a fevered forehead
Knowing how to measure a belly's symmetry
kneading the narah pains away

Once my baby sister stuffed
a split-pea up her nostril
my mother got a crochet needle
and gently tried to pry it out

We stood around her
like inquisitive gauldings

Suddenly, in surgeon's tone she ordered,
'Pass the black pepper,'
and patted a little
under the dozing nose

My baby sister sneezed.
The rest was history.

Out of Africa

Out of Africa of the suckling
Out of Africa of the tired woman in earrings
Out of Africa of the black-foot leap
Out of Africa of the baobab, the suck-teeth
Out of Africa of the dry maw of hunger
Out of Africa of the first rains, the first mother.

Into the Caribbean of the staggeringly blue sea-eye
Into the Caribbean of the baleful tourist glare
Into the Caribbean of the hurricane
Into the Caribbean of the flame tree, the palm tree,
the ackee, the high smelling saltfish
and the happy creole so-called mentality.

Into England of the frost and the tea
Into England of the budgie and the strawberry
Into England of the trampled autumn tongues
Into England of the meagre funerals
Into England of the hand of the old woman
And the gent running behind someone
who's forgotten their umbrella, crying out,
'I say . . . I say-ay.'

Configurations

He gives her all the configurations
of Europe.

She gives him a cloud burst of parrots.

He gives her straight blond hairs
and a white frenzy.

She gives him black wool. The darkness
of her twin fruits.

He gives her uranium, platinum, aluminium
and concorde.

She gives him her 'Bantu buttocks'.

He rants about the spice in her skin.

She croons his alabaster and scratches him.

He does a Columbus –
falling on the shores of her tangled nappy orchard.

She delivers up the whole Indies again
But this time her wide legs close in
      slowly
Making a golden stool of the empire
of his head.

Always Potential

Articulated lorries
streaming up the North Circular,
streaming like profit
big brand names flashing by;
KODAK, JOHNSON'S, CADBURY,
triggering a bell of sugarcane
somewhere in my head.

The smell of sausages and eggs
from the Transport Cafe,
the egg-on-toast and tea
leaving a queer taste of aluminium
in my mouth.
Queer as the hills
of unsmeltered bauxite
in my raw underdeveloped country.

And I can hear
the back home politician-drone
'We have a lot of potential
a lot of potential.'

Always potential.

*There is no Centre of the Universe**

And though
butter mountains
cheese mountains
beef mountains
can give a country
a certain air
like a nuclear base
or reserved space claim
butter mountains
cheese mountains
beef mountains
can't offer any peaks
to wonderment
can only be a bulk
in the eye
a civilised cataract
lying between
the central vision
and the central issue
of a child's famined heart.

* Alice Walker, *In Search of Our Mothers' Gardens*

33

Cosmic Spite

We, the people, 'third in the world'
Feet courting the sands and mud
Of natural disasters.
After the hurricane, the floods, the famines,
The droughts and foreign debts
We chew the biblical philosophy wonderingly –
To him that hath even more will be given
To him that hath not . . .
But we keep on stirring rich dreams
Into the groundy porridge for our children
We keep on – the rhythm of our hard sweet lives
Despite the cosmic spite.

Beverley's Saga

(For Beverley and Jamaican dub-poet, Jean Binta Breeze)

Me good friend Beverley
Come to England. She was three.
She born in Jamaica, but seh,
Dis ya she country.
She ancestor blood help fe build it,
Dat is history.
Dih black presence go back
Two, three century.

She seh she fadder
Was minding he own business
Back in Jam-country,
Wid he lickle piece-o-land
An he lickle donkey
When dey sen he fe enlist
In de British Army.
Yes, he hads was to fight
Fe dis ya country.
Dey even give he medal fe bravery.

So policeman na come
Wid no brutality.
Mister Repatriation, yuh know,
You will haffi kill she
Cause she na go no whey
Dis ya she country.
Summer is hearts
An she dread de wintry
But she have she lickle flat
An she have she lickle key.

She seh she like it fine
She a pop wid style
You can never put she back inna no woodpile
Or she bun it to de ground.

She seh she went to Uncle Sam
For a six-week vacation,
But after three week
She homesick fe England.
When de plane mek a touch-down
She feel so happy,
She feel she a come home,
Dis ya she country.
If dey think bout repatriation
Dem will haffi kill she.

De odder day
Wan ole English lady stop she,
Seh, 'Miss are you on holiday?'
Bev seh, 'Me not on holiday,
Me a live right hey.
Me na plan fe go no whey.'

De ole lady open she eye, surprisedly,
Bev seh, 'Is Black British dey call we.'
She seh, 'I don't mean to be unkind
But leh me tell you lickle history —
You see all dis big fat architectry?
In it is de blood of my ancestry.
Dih black presence go back
Two, three century.
Don't look at me so bemusedly.'

Bev seh, 'In any case, you been my country first,
So we come back inna kinda reverse.
Isn't life funny? Dis ya. Dis ya history.
O mek we tek a lickle walk,
It so nice an sunny.
Summer is hearts,
An a dread de wintry.
But a have me lickle flat
An a have me lickle key.
You want to come in
For a lickle cup-o-tea?'

Break/Dance

(After watching Lesley break/dancing on the carpet,
and remembering the young black break/dancers around Covent Garden)

I'm going to break/dance
turn rippling glass
stretch my muscles
to the bass
Ooooh I'm **going** to break/dance

I'm going to rip it
and jerk it
and tear it apart
I'm going to chop it
and move it
and groove it

Oooh I'm going to ooze it
electric boogaloo
electric boogaloo
across your floor
I'm going to break/dance
watch my ass
take the shine off your laugh

Ooooh I'm going to dip it
and spin it
let my spine twist it
I'm going to shift it
and stride it
let my mind glide it

Then I'm going to ease it
Ease it, and bring it all home

Believing in the beat
Believing in the beat
Of MY SELF.

Walking With My Brother
in Georgetown

(August 1984)

Dih city dying
dih trenches seem smaller
dih streets
dih houses
an everyting an everybody
look suh rundown
an stamp wid dih dry ah hunger

You been away too long girl
smile mih brudder

Dih city dying
we need a purging
new fires burning
some incense
dih sun too indifferent

You been away too long girl
smile mih brudder

An ah hearing dub-music blaring
An ah seeing dih man-youths rocking
Hypnosis on dih streets
Rocking to dih rhythm of dere own deaths
Locked in a shop-front beat

You been away too long girl
smile mih brudder

Dih city dying
we need new blooding
an boning
too many deaths unmourning
Jonestown, Walter
time like it ground still

Hibiscus blooming
People grooving
Girl, why yuh sehing dih city dying
Seh me brudder sighing

Maybe I lying
Maybe I dying.

Emerald Heart

But I have journeyed deep
into the emerald heart
of my country

Slept at mountaintop
with the curled knowledge
that Kanaima* could devour my sleep

I ate labba*
drank creek water
waded up to my knees
through all the vast harshness
the irredeemable beauty

Like a simple peasant woman
I weep
for all the harvests
that could have been.

* Kanaima – Amerindian figure of death.
* There's an old Guyanese belief that if you eat
labba (wild meat) and drink creek water, you
will return to Guyana.

Child-Kingdom

Now I return to my child-kingdom
To my brownwater house of many mansions
To my green and sunbaked pasturelands

How I crouched on the small of my days then
Framed in the plasmic eye of a patwa
The constant O-ing of the little fish mouth
The groggy fish-eye taking me out

How I bit into green guavas then
Belly-binding
Dress strap hanging, a little like
A beggar-maid princess

And cows sang for me
Donkeys heralded me
Sheep parted at my coming

And I was God-child
To all the brown waters
I surveyed.

(Three For Children)

Granny Granny Please Comb
My Hair

Granny Granny please comb
my hair
you always take your time
you always take such care

You put me on a cushion
between your knees
you rub a little coconut oil
parting gentle as a breeze

Mummy Mummy
she's always in a hurry-hurry
rush
she pulls my hair
sometimes she tugs

But Granny
you have all the time
in the world
and when you're finished
you always turn my head and say
'Now who's a nice girl?'

Wha Me Mudder Do

Mek me tell you wha me Mudder do
wha me mudder do
wha me mudder do

Me mudder pound plantain mek fufu
Me mudder catch crab mek calaloo stew

Mek me tell you wha me mudder do
wha me mudder do
wha me mudder do

Me mudder beat hammer
Me mudder turn screw
she paint chair red
then she paint it blue

Mek me tell you wha me mudder do
wha me mudder do
wha me mudder do

Me mudder chase bad-cow
with one 'Shoo'
she paddle down river
in she own canoe
Ain't have nothing
dat me mudder can't do
Ain't have nothing
dat me mudder can't do

Mek me tell you

For Forest

Forest could keep secrets
Forest could keep secrets

Forest tune in everyday
to watersound and birdsound
Forest letting her hair down
to the teeming creeping of her forest-ground

But Forest don't broadcast her business
no Forest cover her business down
from sky and fast-eye sun
and when night come
and darkness wrap her like a gown
Forest is a bad dream woman

Forest dreaming about mountain
and when earth was young
Forest dreaming of the caress of gold
Forest rootsing with mysterious eldorado

and when howler monkey
wake her up with howl
Forest just stretch and stir
to a new day of sound

but coming back to secrets
Forest could keep secrets
Forest could keep secrets
        And we must keep Forest

On Her Way to Recovery

My thirteen-year-old daughter
is now taller than me.
Illness seemed to have stretched her a bit.

She, who was on her back
for four days and four nights,
feverish, heavy limbed, uneating,

Got up this morning
pulled on her sneakers, my long red dressing gown,
and went out into the garden.

'Don't worry,' she says,
coming suddenly into the room
where I'm lying, 'I dressed warm.'

Startled. Pleased.
I glance up at the red-robed gazelle
on her way to recovery.

Conkers

Autumn treasures
from the horsechestnut tree

Lying roly poly
among their split green casings

Shiny and hard
like pops of polished mahogany

An English schoolboy
picking them up –

The same compulsive
fickle avidity –

As I picked up
orange-coloured cockles

Way back then
from a tropical childhood tree

Hand about to close in . . .
then spotting another even better

Now, waiting on our bus
we grown-ups watch him

Not knowing how or why
we've lost our instinct

For gathering
the magic shed of trees

Though in partyful mood
in wineful spirits

We dance around crying,
'Give me back my conker.'

A Poem for Us

Today I'm going to make a poem for us

I get out the big ware bowl
and wooden spoon

I reach for the flour in the box
that says; GARDEN OF EDEN
(Before the advent of the Serpent)

I add the simple awara-seed ring you gave
the granite and rainbow miracle
still amazing me

I add our butter love
I add your chain
(it makes a hell of a rattle)

I find the tightly screwed down bottle
with my woman howl
The container with your man pain

Now I'm a dealer in mud and water
Now I'm a dealer in mud and water
Giving shape
              Giving shape to our unborn
The child who watches us from some place.
Who is both happy and sad. Watching us.

With Glenda in Brixton Park

She's taking me to feed the ducks,
walking with jaunty
heavy-booted little footsteps
against the elements, her baby
snug as a caterpillar
in the reaches of the pram.
I clutch the paperbag of passed-over bread.

At the park,
we cast our bread like fate,
but always, the small white birds,
hovering above the slow pond-ducks,
get there first, snipping each piece up.

'The white birds are vicious little things,'
she says, as we move on.
I glance quickly at the new-found fortitude
on her face,

And suddenly
she is swimming in her own eye

clothesless
husbandless
babyless

Her dark limbs
hitting once more
the blue Caribbean sea.

De Man

(For James Berry, Jamaican Poet)

De man is a walking tree
him roots strike deep
him trunk stan tall
him branches spread wide-wide
an know a lot a different breeze

De man is a walking tree
long time now him pick himself up
an drag him roots cross wata
drag him roots pass drought,
round stone

An de man mus had fe
pull de weeds o prejudice
from him paths
lif de vines of bitta-ness from him bark
shake off de dross an frost

De man mus had fe stubborn bad
persisting in him own blue-foot dance

An now de man is like a mothering man tree
who know de ways of reviving trampled seeds
washing dem in de milk of encouragement
prodding up de younga trees
saying, 'freedom is nat a merging wid shadows.'

Lashing dem wid de leaves
of him tongue

But na badda what him say
Na badda what him say
De man will represent you
An mo important we will represent him.

Mystery

Mystery, it was a mystery to me
dih way Miss Sheila
chocolate queen of dih rundown
tumbledown tenement yard
come back cool-cool from Uncle Sam
to live with her ruin-face
one-time criminal man

Hardly going any place
only showing smiling window face

Rumour had it in dih yard
dat she was dih one
to dash dih acid pon dih man
then up and leave for Uncle Sam

Rumour had it in dih yard
how she come back of she own accord
typee-love bring she back
without a word, yes Lord

Rumour had it in dih yard
dat he must work some obeah pon her

Mystery, it was a mystery to me
dih way Miss Sheila
chocolate queen of dih rundown
tumbledown tenement yard
just come back cool-cool from Uncle Sam
to live with her ruin-face
one-time criminal man.

Of Course When They Ask for Poems About the 'Realities' of Black Women

What they really want
at times
is a specimen
whose heart is in the dust

A mother-of-sufferer
trampled, oppressed
they want a little black blood
undressed
and validation
for the abused stereotype
already in their heads

Or else they want
a perfect song

I say I can write
no poem big enough
to hold the essence
     of a black woman
     or a white woman
     or a green woman

And there are black women
and black women
like a contrasting sky
of rainbow spectrum

Touch a black woman
you mistake for a rock
and feel her melting
down to fudge

Cradle a soft black woman
and burn fingers as you trace
revolution
beneath her woolly hair

And yes we cut bush
to clear paths
for our children
and yes,
we throw sprat
to catch whale
and yes,
if need be we'll trade
a piece-a-pussy
than see the pickney dem
in de grip-a-hungry-belly

Still, there ain't no
easy-belly category
        for a black woman
        or a white woman
        or a green woman

And there are black women
strong and eloquent
and focused

And there are black women
who somehow always manage to end up
frail victim

And there are black women
considered so dangerous
in South Africa
they prison them away

Maybe this poem is to say,
that I like to see
we black women
full-of-we-selves walking

Crushing out
with each dancing step
the twisted self-negating
history
we've inherited
        Crushing out
        with each dancing step.

Behind the Mask

Soon we must make a journey
behind the mask.
Into the heart. Wherever the spiral memory
leads our dreaming feet.

And we will move like a host
and who will stop our coming?
Who will stop our lingering
in the teeming market places,
The meditation of fabric
between finger and thumb?

And we will strike soft bargains
And Merone, Oyo and Timbuctoo
will be like fruits in our mouths.
And we will stroll the shores of Benin
and contemplate its meaning.

And we will move on.
And the soles of our feet
will sing to the sands
and the sacred serpents of the desert
will dance.

And some sea will part again
at our coming.

And we will drink up the Niger
and the Nile
and help each other pick the lies
from out our Kushite hair.

And we will stoop to find
the stones we left buried,
the small smooth ones
which are still warm.

Which still carry within them
the memory
of our fondest secrets.

Tapestry

The long line of blood
and family ties

An African countenance here
A European countenance there
An Amerindian cast of cheek
An Asianic turn of eye
And the tongue's salty accommodation
The tapestry is mine
All the bloodstained prints
The scatterlinks
The grafting strand of crinkled hair
The black persistent blooming.

ALSO BY GRACE NICHOLS

The Fat Black Woman's Poems

'Not only rich music, an easy lyricism, but also grit and earthy honesty, a willingness to be vulnerable and clean'
— *Gwendolyn Brooks*

Grace Nichols gives us images that stare us straight in the eye, images of joy, challenge, accusation. Her 'fat black woman' is brash; rejoices in herself; poses awkward questions to politicians, rulers, suitors, to a white world that still turns its back. In the other sequences of this collection, Grace Nichols writes in a language that is wonderfully vivid yet economical, of the pleasures and sadnesses of memory, of loving, of 'the power to be what I am, a woman, charting my own futures'.